Do You Trust Me?

Mark Joseph Young

Contents

Introduction

For by grace you have been saved through faith....[1]

It did not start two years ago,[2] but it started to come into focus then.   I had turned my attention back to Paul's Epistle to the Romans, thinking then that I was going to have the opportunity once more to teach that great work to undergraduates[3] and realizing that my notes were lost or destroyed and would have to be rebuilt.   As I worked my way through the book, the emphasis on faith came through, and I thought more about it.[4]

It had been some time prior to this that I had been back in Genesis, and had given considerable attention to those dawn of time stories.   What was happening with Adam and Eve, with Cain and Abel?   What was God really saying there?   As I turned that over in my mind, I had begun to see, perhaps at last, what the New Testament authors kept saying, that justification by faith was not God's new way, but the way God had always dealt with man from the beginning of time, the way he dealt

---

[1] Ephesians 2:8

[2] In the summer of 2004.

[3] I had taught Romans to undergraduate students at The Institute of the Great Commission in Pitman, New Jersey, in the early 1980s.   The opportunity to teach in another classroom did not materialize, but instead the Christian Gamers Guild's online Chaplain's Bible Study began shortly thereafter.

[4] My *Romans Analytical Study* is the primary result of this study, currently available only at the aforementioned Bible study series.

1

with Abraham and David, and even with Abel. I saw those stories with a fresh eye, the eye that could perceive why they were about faith all along, and why so many missed that.

In the midst of this, I recalled an image from the Disney movie *Aladdin*; it presented the picture that captured the truth. Aladdin reaches out his hand to the princess and says, "Do you trust me?" Hesitantly she replies, "Yes." That, I realized, was how God was reaching out to man, asking, "Do you trust me?" Like Aladdin, all He needs is that hesitant, "Yes," and He will take it from there.

In the movie, Aladdin next says, "Then jump," and off they go on a wild escape. Perhaps that, too, is what God says to us: if you trust Me, jump. Put yourself entirely in my hands. Believe that what I tell you to do is the best thing for you to do. Jump. Yet even so, jumping is not faith; it is the proof of faith. I had been pushed not to a deeper but to a simpler understanding of the notion.

For many people I knew, this would be unacceptable. Faith, for some, was a matter of intellectually embracing correct doctrine, knowing the formula for the Trinity, recognizing the combined divinity and humanity of Christ, believing the right things about baptism and communion, the right theories of justification and sanctification, and attending to the appropriate rituals. For others, it was an emotion, something that you worked up by trying hard to feel like you believed.

If I am right, though, those images of faith are false and misleading. If faith is no more than putting your hand in the hand that reaches toward you, and saying, "Yes, I trust you," it is fundamentally different from what most Christians and nearly all non-Christians understand it to be. It changes how we view our salvation, our sanctification, everything.

Because it changes everything, it is essential that we know whether it is right. It is not enough that I say it is right. It is not enough that I claim the support of comments here and there through history from theological authors whose words appear to assert the same. You must see from scripture what I believe Paul saw, that everything comes back to whether you trust God.

That is why this book was written.

My first book on Christian life, *What Does God Expect? A Gospel-based Approach to Christian Conduct*, was the book I felt compelled to write. It had to be written, and it came into a coherent whole (incorporating some previously published material I had never imagined as part of a larger work) in a matter of days. By contrast, *About the Fruit* was my wife's suggestion. I had gotten a fair amount of mail about a short teaching I had done on that subject, and she thought a book taking the ideas further (already they had expanded since that first teaching had been given) would be well-received. It was a labor of love, but a labor none the less, as I put much prayer and work over many months into understanding and expressing the concepts it contained. This book fell somewhere between the two. I had shared and even taught many of the elements quite independently of each other, but had known they fit together. My *Quick Word* radio show[5] needed a new topic, and the idea of presenting this simple understanding of faith as trusting God would not let me go. While I was drafting those scripts and recording them, I determined that a more complete consideration of the concept in book form for a wider audience was needed, and began writing this.

As I began to write it, all of life conspired to test what I thought. Did I truly trust God, the way I saw in the Bible? What did it mean, and what did it demand of me? Those lessons, too, have added something to this book. Then once it was written, it demanded to be published. Rarely did a week pass without someone asking me a question to which the answer was in this book. I found myself copying sections and even chapters into responses, and realized just how needed the book was. This drew me back to it, pushing to get it polished and printed even before the reviews were back from the last book. What had started more as a way of collecting my thoughts on a subject proved to be an important explanation of core elements of our religion, things we all should have been told few seemed to grasp.

The first edition of this book was published and announced to a close circle of friends and acquaintances, but never properly promoted; it languished until something went wrong with its publication. Dimensionfold Books graciously offered to put it back in print in this second edition, which has a few minor corrections I had intended to

---

[5] At that time on the Lift FM radio stations in Hopewell Township and Rio Grande, NJ, and over the Internet.

make previously and never managed to incorporate. There are many people I could and should thank for their contributions to this book and my understanding of all it contains, and I trust that they will forgive not being named individually. I would like to thank my daughter-in-law, Kellie Young, for the original front cover image, which I thought captured the vision I had; this edition attempts to capture the same vision in an updated image that the publisher felt would be more marketable today. Also, ten years ago my works were all published under the nom de plume "M. Joseph Young", but with the release of my newer books[6] Dimensionfold wanted to use my full name, and thus this is published under the name "Mark Joseph Young".

It is my hope and prayer that it benefits you, opening your eyes not to new depths but to new simplicities in what it is to believe.

--M. Joseph Young

---

[6] The newer books are *Why I Believe* and *The Essential Guide to Time Travel*, both from Dimensionfold Books.

Faith and Knowing

Now faith is the assurance of things hoped for, the conviction of things not seen.[7]

The book we call Hebrews contains a chapter in which faith is discussed, and many Old Testament heroes are named as examples. This eleventh chapter of the book opens with a definition of faith cited by many but not terribly well understood. We imagine faith to be some supernatural ability, but consideration of the matter will show that it is the most natural thing in the world, something we do every day, a thousand times a day, from the moment we awaken.

The first thing contained in the definition is *the assurance of things hoped*. That is, faith is how we know things we don't really know but only hope are so.

When I get out of bed in the middle of the night, I don't generally look to see if my slippers are there; I reach out with my feet to find them. I leave them by my bed when I lie down, and expect them to be there later. Of course, it is possible that my wife, or the dog, or one of the kids, will have moved them—pushed them under the bed, perhaps. Yet I expect them to be there, and usually they are. More significantly, I don't check whether the floor is there. That may sound silly, but people have slept through disasters, waking up to find their homes in ruins around them. I do not really know that the

---

[7] Hebrews 11:1, New American Standard Version

floor is still there. I only hope that it is there, and believe that it is there. I have faith that the floor is there, and that faith assures me that what I hope is true.

Once you understand faith this way, you begin to recognize it in everything in your daily life. You put the food away in the refrigerator at night and expect to find it there in the morning. If you have teenaged sons, this might be faith ill-placed, but it is still your expectation. You write checks, expecting that the money you deposited in the bank will be there to cover them when they are presented. You believe that the clothes in your drawer and closet will be clean, that the cash in your pocket will still be accepted at the store when you buy coffee in the morning, that your employer will be in business and that the check he gives you on payday will be good. You have faith that the food you buy in the grocery store is safe to eat, that the other drivers on the road are mostly sober and sane and law-abiding. You expect your car to start, your phone to work, your electricity to be there. You believe that your front steps will support your weight, and that your clothes will still fit. You know none of these things. Every one of them could be wrong, and sometimes for some people they are wrong. However, you cannot go through life checking everything all the time, and so you rely by faith that things will be right.

Christian faith is like this. You don't check whether God is there; you simply assume that He is there and act accordingly. Like stepping out of bed without looking for the floor, you trust that God will be there.

The verse does not end there, though. It gives us another definition of faith, which is really the same faculty in a different context. It tells us that faith is *the conviction of things not seen*. That is, once again, faith is how we know things we don't know, but this time it's not things that we simply don't check, but things we cannot check, things we cannot know of our own knowledge. I hope the car will start; I believe the car will start. When I turn the key, I find out whether the car starts. When I get out of bed, I trust that the floor is there, but if I had any doubt I could look. However, the conviction of things not seen is how we know what we cannot check for ourselves. This, too, is an essential faculty. In fact, most of what you think you know you only know by faith. Permit me to illustrate it.

Have you ever met George Washington? Perhaps more specifically, did you visit him when he was at Valley Forge? Undoubtedly someone told you who George Washington was, and that he camped at Valley Forge, and you believed it. Have you been to London, Paris, Moscow, Beijing, Tokyo, Taipei, Sydney, Honolulu, San Francisco, New Orleans, Chicago, New York, and McMurdo[8]? Very few people have actually been to all of those places; I certainly have not. You only know those places are real because you believed what you were told. Someone told you about them, and you trusted what they said.

---

[8] A small community mostly of researchers on Ross Island in Antarctica

I have been to New York. New York is real; you can take my word for it. Yet if you do, you will not really know, of your own knowledge, that New York is real. You only believe it is real because I told you that it was—the conviction of things not seen. You might have seen New York in a movie, but how do you know it was not a movie set? You've undoubtedly seen photographs, but they could have been of models. Unless you have been to New York yourself, your knowledge of the city is based entirely on your faith, the faith that what you were told is true. Even if you have been there, you still are basing your knowledge on faith, faith in the information that led you to believe that this was, in reality, New York, and not some other place masquerading as that city.

Once you understand this definition of faith, you should realize that most of what you think you know, and nearly all of what you call your education, you know by faith. You know that atomic clocks exist, and that time slows as you approach the speed of light, because you were told; very few people have actually conducted experiments that demonstrate time dilation, and the rest of us believe their statements that they watched it happen. Faith is the basis for anything you claim to know that you never actually saw for yourself.

Faith is how most of us first knew that Jesus rose from the grave. Someone told us; we read it in the pages of the Bible. We had no reason to doubt what we read, what we were told. We believed it, because we trusted the people who told us.

Of course, this kind of faith can be wrong, too. The people who told us might have been mistaken. At one time many people believed that the world was flat. Even those who knew that the world was round for a very long time believed that the sun went around the earth. This knowledge was passed from teacher to student, and accepted by faith. It was wrong. We do not escape the possibility that we might believe something that is not true. Many people have been told that role playing games such as *Dungeons & Dragons*™ are somehow connected to witchcraft and Satanism. These people were told this by people they trusted, people who had never been wrong about anything that mattered. Yet it is not true. The fact is the creators of that original role playing game were Christians.[9] *Dungeons & Dragons*™ turns out to be one of the most Christian games around today. Unfortunately, many Christians have accepted by faith a lie about it. There are many things people know by faith that are not true. George Washington did not chop down a cherry tree; that was a children's story written after his death to illustrate the importance of honesty. The signers of the Declaration of Independence were not all Christians trying to create a Christian nation; they were gentlemen of the Enlightenment, who believed in the ultimate nature of Reason, quite a few of them deists who denied the incarnation. You can have the conviction of things not seen and be mistaken.

---

[9] Prior to their deaths, Dave Arneson was a Christian for many years, and an elder in his church, and E. Gary Gygax also professed Christian faith, and was a serious student of scripture, although not connected with any particular denomination.

11

Yet these two natural functions of our minds are definitive of faith. We have faith when we act as if something is true simply because we expect it to be true, and we have faith when we believe we know something we have never seen for ourselves.

It is from this that the writer of Hebrews concludes that we know by faith that the worlds were made from that which is invisible, by the word of God.[10] We were not there. No one was there but God, as far as we know. God told someone, perhaps Adam, perhaps Moses, certainly not me, that He made the world by speaking it into existence. We have faith that the world came into existence by God's decree. We were told that God said it. We have faith that the people who told us got it right.

This is the starting point, the essential understanding of what faith is. It is not something you have only when God gives it to you, but something you have and use all the time. It is not something you have to feel, but something that is a natural cognitive function. It is not an intellectual agreement with a list of doctrinal statements, but reliance on truths which you cannot genuinely know.

From here, we have to examine how that works in relation to God.

---

[10] Hebrews 11:3

12

The Loss of Trust

I heard the sound of You in the Garden, and I was afraid....[11]

Although Hebrews names many Old Testament people who had faith, the first person we need to consider is not mentioned. He is not an example of faith, but proves in fact to be the ultimate demonstration of not having faith. In the third chapter of Genesis we read about the fall, and the sin of our father Adam.

The fascinating thing about this passage is the clothes. They are mentioned, one way or another, repeatedly. We are told first that Adam and Eve were naked and unashamed,[12] that it did not bother them to be naked. Then, as soon as they had eaten the fruit of the tree of the knowledge of good and evil, they saw that they were naked, and immediately they attempted to clothe themselves.[13] After that, when God asked why they were hiding, Adam said it was because they were naked, and God asked how they knew this.[14] In the end, God gave them clothes,[15] and sent them out of the garden.[16] What is the point about the clothes?

The first guess we might make is that it was evil for Adam and Eve to be naked, but they did not

---

[11] Genesis 3:10
[12] Genesis 2:25
[13] Genesis 3:7
[14] Genesis 3:11
[15] Genesis 3:21
[16] Genesis 3:23

know this until they gained the knowledge of good and evil, and then they had to find clothes, because putting on clothes was good. This cannot be so, though, because God made them naked. God could not have made them naked if being naked was evil; besides, God saw that it was good. Everything God made was good.[17]

Then it must be, we guess, that the act of clothing themselves was evil, and that we ought to abandon our clothes and return to being naked and good. Since having the knowledge of good and evil was the only thing they got from the tree, and being naked was good, being clothed must be evil. Alas, this does not work either, because God made clothes for them, and if the clothes were evil, God could not have given them clothes.

It seems, then, that the clothes are irrelevant. It is not evil to be naked, and it is not evil to be clothed. Yet the clothes seem to be the salient point, the part that is mentioned repeatedly. If they are irrelevant, why are they even mentioned? Somehow they seem to matter; the entire passage seems to be about Adam's sudden need to be clothed. How can this be?

It must be that when Adam gained the knowledge of good and evil, he realized something about being naked. Up to this point, Adam had never considered whether his actions were good or evil; he did what he did. Now, though, he must have recognized that some things he could do would be good, and some would be evil. That is, there

---

[17] Genesis 1:31

were things he could do to Eve that would be nice, caring, beneficial for Eve, but there were also things he could do that would hurt her, and possibly hurt her very badly. For the first time in his life, he realized he was dangerous. He could hurt Eve, the animals, the garden—he could do evil.

It must then have occurred to him that Eve was also dangerous. She in fact could hurt him, and hurt him as badly as he could hurt her. The animals, too, were dangerous.

For us, clothes are such a natural part of life that we never really consider what they do. All clothes exist primarily to protect us, to shield us from the elements, to guard our skin against abrasion, to keep us warm, and to protect us from each other. This aspect of the nature of clothes is particularly emphasized when we consider specialized garments, the clothes worn by firefighters or hazardous materials teams or medical professionals. We wear clothes for protection.

What Adam realized, what caused him to don clothes, was that he was vulnerable. He needed to protect himself against Eve, against the animals, against others who could hurt him. He did his best to provide this protection for himself, using leaves.

However, no garment could protect Adam from God. God was the ultimate danger. He could hurt Adam very badly, and there was nothing Adam could do to protect himself from God, and nothing he could do to threaten retaliation against God. God could hurt him, and he could not hurt God. Thus when God came back, Adam hid himself.[18]

Notice what Adam says. He tells God that he hid himself because he was *afraid*.[19] He does not say he was embarrassed or ashamed. He was afraid. He realized that God could hurt him, and—here is the critical point—*he did not trust God*. He knew that God could destroy him, and he had no reason to believe that God would not do what God could do. Now that he knew what evil was, he thought God was capable of it.

Adam had to leave the garden. It was not possible for him to feel safe in God's garden, once he thought God might hurt him. Not even the clothes God gave him would make him safe. That trust, that faith, was gone, and Adam never got it back.

However, one of his sons did.

---

[18] Genesis 3:8
[19] Genesis 3:10, New American Standard Bible

A Sacrifice by Faith

By faith Abel offered to God a better sacrifice than Cain....[20]

The first person mentioned in the eleventh chapter of Hebrews as an example of faith is Abel, the second son of Adam and Eve. Our attention is called to the fourth chapter of Genesis, an account in which the two brothers each brought a sacrifice to God, but Cain's was rejected and Abel's was accepted. The author of Hebrews tells us that Abel's sacrifice was accepted because of his faith. Yet if you read that chapter, you will find no mention of Abel's faith. What was it that made Abel's sacrifice better than Cain's, and how did the author of Hebrews recognize that as faith?

You will hear much speculation about the reasons for God accepting Abel but not Cain. Some say that it was because Cain brought *some* of his crops but Abel brought the first fruits; however, the text says that Abel *also* brought his first fruits,[21] and that means he brought the first fruits just as Cain had done. Some say it is because Abel's sacrifice had blood in it and Cain's did not. However, there has been nothing to this point to suggest that the boys should have known blood would matter, blood is not mentioned in the entire passage, and many times hereafter God accepts sacrifices of crops, so this is grasping at straws. Besides, if it is about what is in the sacrifice itself, it is works—doing the

---

[20] Hebrews 11:4
[21] Genesis 4:4

right thing—that made Abel's sacrifice acceptable. Some say that we can see that God rejected Cain because God knew Cain's attitude would be bad if he were rejected, but what do we really know? Would Abel have reacted badly had God rejected him? None of these ideas are particularly well supported by the text, and none of them have anything to do with faith as the critical issue. You can read the fourth chapter of Genesis a hundred times, and not find any reason for God to have rejected Cain's sacrifice.

The answer is actually in the *third* chapter of Genesis. This is what the author of Hebrews saw that told him that Abel came to God by faith, and Cain did not.

When God sent Adam out of the Garden, God decreed a law. That law stated that Adam and his descendants were to scratch their food out of the dirt, growing crops by the sweat of their brows.[22] They were to be vegetarians, agrarian people cultivating the land.

Cain brought to God a sacrifice of crops he had grown by his own labor.[23] He was keeping that law. He was doing what God had commanded. His sacrifice said, "God, I have done everything you commanded, so you must accept me, because I am good."

---

[22] Genesis 3:17ff
[23] Genesis 4:3

Abel, though, is not farming the land. We are told that he is raising livestock.[24] Any Israelite herdsman could tell you that if you raise livestock, you eat the meat. That's the point of raising it. God didn't say that they should or could eat meat. He told them to eat the crops they grew in the ground. The Jewish nomads Moses led out of Egypt would have realized immediately that Abel was disobeying that law. He was eating meat.

Christian theologians seem very confused about this. Many will tell you that Abel was not eating meat. They base this on the fact that Abel's sacrifice was accepted, and therefore they conclude he must have been righteous, and that he could not have been righteous if he were breaking the law by eating the meat that God did not permit men to eat.[25] God could not have accepted the sacrifice of a sinful meat-eater. Abel must have been eating dairy products, milk and cheese,[26] perhaps also foraging for wild vegetables, and perhaps trading the wool and milk of his beasts to Cain for a share of the produce. However, the text very nearly tells us that this is wrong, that Abel was eating meat.

---

[24] Genesis 4:2
[25] God does not authorize eating meat until after the flood, in Genesis 9:3
[26] The idea that Abel ate dairy products but not meat does not relieve the difficulty here. Our modern conceptions hold that it is a choice between eating meat and not eating meat, but the instructions to Adam did not mention meat, instead focusing on crops as the only acceptable source. Even if it is insisted that Abel ate dairy products but not meat, he is still breaking this law.

If you look, you will see that Abel offered to God *the fat portions*.[27] This tells us three things that are really the same thing told three ways. In order for Abel to offer God the fat portions, he had to know how to butcher meat. He had to cut up that animal and separate this delicious portion as God's share. Why would a herdsman know how to cut up meat unless it was something he did regularly? That it is the delicious portion is evident. The fat portions are the part people like. They are more tender, more juicy. They cook better. Why, though, would Abel offer God the fat portions, unless he already knew that that was the tasty part? Finally, why offer to God the fat portions instead of the entire beast? What did he do with the rest? The obvious answer is that he ate it. He gave God the best part of the meat, but he ate the rest himself.

Suddenly we have the two brothers in stark contrast. Cain is the legally righteous one, the one who has kept God's commandments, who can bring his offering to God and say, "See, I have done what you require, and you must accept me." His brother, though, brings a sacrifice that screams disobedience. His very sacrifice says, "I have flaunted every rule you made, disobeyed in every way, but I am bringing this to you in the hope that you will have mercy and receive me anyway."

That is what the author of Hebrews saw. That is why Abel's sacrifice is one of faith. Right here, at the dawn of time, we have the conflict between faith and works put in stark contrast. The one brother attempts to claim God's blessing based

---

[27] Genesis 4:4

on his own meritorious conduct. The other comes to beg for mercy for his sin. It is the sinful brother who is accepted, not because he is sinful but because he makes no pretense of righteousness. He comes not to claim his rights but to ask for mercy.

It is he who truly trusts God. Cain is trying to manipulate God, to use God's rules against him, to make God treat him well by using God's words against Him. Abel is the one who says, "I dare to come to You, You who could and should destroy me, and to believe that You will not destroy me, but that You care enough about me to receive me and be merciful, to treat me as I do not deserve, to love me despite the fact that I am nothing You said You wanted me to be, other than a man who knows that he needs You."

In short, Cain thought God was the sort of being who might destroy you if you didn't do the right things to protect yourself from Him, and Abel thought God was the sort of being you could trust to be kind even if you did not deserve it. That was the difference between them, and the difference between their sacrifices, and that is why Abel is an example of faith.

The Father of the Faithful

Abraham believed God, and it was accounted to him as righteousness....[28]

In writing to the Romans, Paul spends a great deal of time examining the faith of Abraham.[29] This man, we are told, is the father of the faithful, the patriarch of the true people of God, the Christians. He is a father of many nations, because we, the gentiles, have joined ourselves to his lineage, and become part of the real Israel. We were able to do that, Paul says, because we have the same kind of faith that Abraham had.[30]

It makes sense, then, to understand what kind of faith Abraham had, because our faith saves us as his faith saved him, to the degree that our faith is like his faith. Paul points our attention to the fifteenth chapter of Genesis, by quoting a phrase from it: *Abraham believed God, and it was accounted to him as righteousness.*[31] That is, God listed Abraham as righteous because of Abraham's faith; by our faith, we, too, are listed as righteous.

What was it that Abraham believed?

The simple answer to that question doesn't seem to help much. What Abraham believed was that his descendants would be so numerous no one

---

[28] Romans 4:3, Genesis 15:6
[29] Primarily in chapter 4
[30] Romans 4:16
[31] Romans 4:3, Genesis 15:6

could count them.[32] From one perspective this was a silly thing for him to have believed. After all, he and his wife were well past the social security retirement age, and if they'd had any children those offspring would probably have moved them into a nursing home by this point. There comes a time in your life when you decide that children are no longer a possibility. We would not say that Abraham believed the impossible, as pregnancies in elderly couples do happen once in a while, but we would say that this was highly improbable. Yet there is no suggestion in the New Testament that we also are supposed to believe we will have large families. There must be some other aspect of this that applies to us.

That aspect is seen not in what Abraham believed, but in why. Abraham did not wake up one day and ask God to give him a big family, and then believe it was going to happen. Rather, one day God told him that there were going to be all these descendants. "You do know," Abraham said with a bit of a chuckle, "that my wife and I are past childbearing age, don't you?" "It doesn't matter," was God's serious answer. "You are going to have more descendants than you can count."

Remember that the first example in Hebrews of someone whose faith gained him God's acceptance was Abel, who trusted that God would receive him despite his sin. That author also named Enoch,[33] of whom we are told only that he walked with God, and then God took him and no one could

---

[32] Genesis 15:5
[33] Hebrews 11:5f, Genesis 5:21ff

find him on earth anymore. Noah, too, is named,[34] as having had faith enough to build an ark when God told him to do so. Now we are given Abraham. The common thread here is that these men trusted God. Enoch dared to enter God's presence despite being mortal and sinful. Noah constructed a huge boat, believing not only that God would make good on His promise to send rain but would also give him a way to gather the incredible number of wild animals who needed to be preserved on it. Abraham trusted that if God said there would be descendants, he would have heirs for his property. God was not pulling his leg, setting him up for disappointment. He would do what He said.

In other words, it is not so much what you believe as whom you believe. Abraham trusted God.

It is important that we see this. Paul uses Abraham in Romans 4 as the link which allows those who are not God's people by birth to become God's people by faith, and also to exclude from God's people those Israelites who do not have faith. It is not bloodlines that matter, he says. You are not Jewish because your parents were Jewish. You are Jewish because like Abraham you trust God. This, and only this, makes you a member of Abraham's family. Birth does not matter, because Ishmael and Esau were legitimately born in that family but excluded from it. Circumcision does not matter, because Abraham was given the promise decades before he was circumcised. What matters is that we trust God as Abraham trusted God, believing that

---

[34] Hebrews 11:7, Genesis 6:8ff

God will accept us and treat us kindly and lovingly, not cruelly and not even fairly or justly.

The gospel, the concept that we are saved by God's grace in response to our faith, is not a new idea Jesus introduced. It is the same way of salvation that reached back to the dawn of time. Jesus announced it yet again, and made it clearer than it had ever been before, but He was not changing the way to come to God. Abraham was saved by faith; so, too, were Abel, Enoch, Noah, Isaac, Jacob, Joseph, Moses, David, and every other Old Testament saint right up through Mary the Virgin and John the Baptist. None of these were saved by keeping the Law; all were saved because they trusted God and believed that if you came to God hoping for mercy, you would receive mercy.

What Jesus did was provide payment for the penalty, making it possible for God to excuse sin. How He did that is both complicated and debated, but that He did that is clear in scripture. One explanation, in simple terms, says that if someone does wrong, then someone suffers. Justice is about making sure that the person who suffers the wrong is put right at the expense of the person who did the wrong. That is, every harm any of us has ever caused must be borne by someone, and it is unfair for the harm to fall on those we have wronged because, at least in connection with what we have done, they are innocent. Yet if the harm falls on us, we die. Thus God, in offering mercy, has in essence said that He will bear the penalty for our wrongs; He will suffer so that we do not have to. How, though, can God suffer? Jesus became man in order to suffer, because He is God, and when He suffered,

God suffered.   Thus someone suffered for everything you did, and God can excuse you for all you have done.

The Mustard Seed

...if you have faith the size of a mustard seed...nothing will be impossible to you.[35]

How much faith is enough?

An avowed agnostic once wrote to me to say that Christians did not have faith, because they did not trust God completely. In the course of our discussions, he pointed to the passage in Genesis 22,[36] where Abraham puts his son Isaac on the altar as an offering to God. Christians, he asserted, would not be willing to do this.

My correspondent did not truly grasp the ramifications of what Abraham was doing. There is a tale told of a petty king in the medieval age who gave his son as pledge that he would pay tribute to an invader. Later when the other came to collect the tribute and the king refused, the invader threatened to kill the boy. Indicating that he didn't care whether the boy lived or died, the monarch said, "I have the hammer and anvil with which I forged him, and I can forge me another just like him."

It was not so with Isaac. It was not merely that this was the miracle child, the boy who should not have been possible and yet was born all the same. God had said, "Through Isaac shall your descendants be named."[37] All of God's promises depended on Isaac having children of his own, and

---

[35] Matthew 17:20 New American Standard Version
[36] Genesis 22:1-19
[37] Genesis 21:12, Romans 9:7, Hebrews 11:19

29

the boy had no children, no wife, no chance of producing offspring for a few years yet. If Isaac died, God's promises died with him.

We minimize this by making it about Abraham's willingness to kill his own son. It was that, but it was so much more than that. God was asking Abraham not merely whether he loved God more than he loved his child, but whether he loved God more than he loved all that God had promised. Was he willing to sacrifice the wonderful future, the generations of descendants as the sands of the sea, the wealth and fame and respect of history, if God asked him to do that? Did he love God for what God was going to do for him, or did he love God simply for being God?

We also minimize how much Abraham trusted God. We see that despite Isaac being the child of promise, Abraham still placed him on the altar, and prepared to slay him. We have come this far, and so we realize that Abraham was willing to sacrifice not only Isaac but all God had promised. Yet Abraham's faith is bigger than that. The author of Hebrews tells us that Abraham trusted that God was able even to raise Isaac from the dead, if it was necessary.[38]

From one perspective, we can see that Abraham must have believed this. After all, he trusted that God would fulfill his promises. He believed that his descendants through Isaac would number as the stars or the sands, beyond counting. God's promise could not fail. Therefore, if Isaac

---

[38] Hebrews 11:19

died, Isaac would yet live, because it was only through Isaac's life that God could fulfill those promises. God had to resurrect Isaac if Abraham killed him, or God would be a liar; since it is impossible for God to lie, and God had ordered Isaac's death, it followed that God was going to restore the boy to life if the fatal blow fell.

Yet we also know that this is what Abraham believed. We know this because before he climbed that mountain, alone but for his son, with no animal to sacrifice, knowing that he fully intended to slay the boy, he left instructions for his servant. Those instructions stated, in the plural, "we will go up, we will worship, and we will come down."[39] Abraham knew before he went up that mountain that Isaac would return with him, even though he fully intended to kill the boy on that mountain.

So the ramifications of this story are way beyond what my critic suggested. Abraham's faith was much greater merely than a willingness to kill his son if God asked. Abraham was willing to give up all God promised in response to God's request, and yet believed that God would still fulfill those promises by restoring the dead to life if that was what was required. That is the faith Abraham had.

So I must agree with my critic that most Christians do not have that faith. I do not have it myself. Of course, I am not in Abraham's situation, and no promises made to me depend on the lives of my sons, who are already becoming a multitude.

---

[39] Genesis 22:5. I am indebted to Derek Prince for this observation.

Nor do I expect that God would ask of me the same thing he asked of Abraham. That does not mean I do not get asked hard things, even challenged as to whether I love God for Who He is or for what I believe He will give me. I will not, however, be asked to do what Abraham faced. Nor do I expect most Christians would be able to do that, and it is a weak response to the critic that God will not ask this of them, no matter how good my theological reasons for that are. The fact is, most of us do not trust God as Abraham trusted. That can be laid on us as a just accusation.

It does not worry me. God wants us to have faith even as Abraham had faith, but at the same time He treats us as He treated Abraham. He begins small, with that grain of mustard.

When my conversation with this cynic began, he did not start with the example of Abraham. He started with the very philosophical statement that if God is who we claim He is, He must be absolutely trustworthy, and therefore Christians ought to trust Him absolutely. Since we do not trust God absolutely, God must not be Who we claim.

My answer immediately was that our lack of trust is not based on God's failing but on ours, and that it is a perfectly reasonable failing in the circumstances. God does not show up and announce that He is God and we must trust Him absolutely in everything starting right now, and then demand the sacrifice of our only child. He recognizes that anyone could appear and claim to be God. It is entirely reasonable for us to expect proof—not proof that the God who made all things can be trusted (although there is that, to some degree), but proof rather that this person who comes to us is that God, that the claim is valid. It is one thing to trust absolutely that the Creator of all things is completely trustworthy. It is quite another to believe that we, mere mortals, can actually know Who He is. The One Who comes to us claims to be God, and asks for our trust, but it is quite appropriate for us to expect Him to prove that He is trustworthy, that He is Who He claims to be, and that we can indeed trust Him.

Further, it was so with Abraham. God did not find Abraham one day and say, "I am going to make a great nation of you if you are willing to kill your only son, so go do it." In fact, the first thing God said to Abraham was, "Come, see the land which I will show you, which I will give to your descendants."[40] That was all God asked in the first request: leave your home, go this way, and I'll tell you when you get where I want you to be. Trust me that I am taking you to a beautiful place.

God proved Himself in that. He brought Abraham to a land that was in its time lush pasture with plenty of water and good fruit, a place where he lived comfortably and grew rich as a shepherd caring for flocks. God did this. God could be trusted. It was a little thing, really. It involved leaving one pasture land that was starting to get crowded by urban sprawl and heading for another place where you were told there was good pasture. It included a promise that he would one day own

---

[40] Genesis 12:1ff

33

that land. The wealth that he was accumulating suggested it might be so. That wasn't how God eventually gave his descendants the land, but it certainly was encouraging. It was a good land.

Later, God asked him to believe that there would be descendants. This was a bit tougher, and neither Abraham nor Sarah really believed it immediately. They decided to try to make God's promise come true through their own efforts, involving Sarah's slave Hagar as a second wife—a disaster, since as soon as the young servant girl realized she was carrying the heir to the household, she realized that Sarah would have to treat her as she desired, because once that old Abraham died, her boy Ishmael would be in charge, and Sarah would be at her mercy. God, though, pushed the envelope. He told Abraham that Sarah would have a son, as old as she was, and that this would be the heir. That was correct under the systems of the time. The eldest son of the first wife would be the heir, even if the second wife's son was born first. Hagar would never have believed Sarah could have a son; after all, it was that very doubt that made Hagar the second wife. Yet when God told Abraham Sarah would have a son, He also told Abraham to change their names. Abraham, with a single child, was to change his name from Abram, Exalted Father, to Abraham, Father of a Multitude. His wife had been Sarai, the very personal My Princess, but was to become Sarah, the general Princess, the princess of the nation that would come from her.[41] They did this, showing again that they believed God's promise.

---

[41] Genesis 17:5, 15

God again fulfilled His promise. Against all odds, Isaac was born, and born exactly when God said he would be. Sarah was ninety, Abraham a century old, but the baby was the fulfillment of God's promise, and they knew it. It was also the beginning of the promise, the firstborn of the multitude. God was trustworthy.

Thus when God asked Abraham to sacrifice Isaac, to kill the miracle child through whom the descendants would come and the promises would be fulfilled, Abraham and God already had a track record. Abraham knew that God was good at keeping his promises. Abraham knew that if this was what God wanted, the Lord had a plan that would make it work. The promises were not going to fail.

God usually does not come to us one day and tell us to put our lives in His hand in a life-and-death situation. He asks us to trust Him for something seemingly small, to forgive us. That is not so small a thing as it seems to us, for forgiveness is the greatest thing God gives us; yet to us, we do not realize what it costs or what it means. We say all the time that we forgive others, and we believe that we have done so whether it's true or not. It seems small to us to ask God for forgiveness, and so it is easy to trust Him for that. It is easy to trust Him for heaven, too, at least at the moment we turn to Him. After all, we probably won't even think about it again until we're facing death. It doesn't seem that big a deal, to some degree.

That is, it is much more difficult for us to trust God for things in our daily lives. It is difficult sometimes to believe that He guides and protects us, that He cares for us, that He will meet our needs. It is difficult for us to recognize that it is He Who is meeting our needs, particularly when we work to earn our paychecks and think therefore that they are ours when they come, that we have somehow gotten something without Him. God teaches us that He gives us all we have. It is hard sometimes for us to see that.

It is difficult for us to believe that God knows best for us, yet He asks us to trust Him in this, as well. He offers to guide us to that perfect place for us, just as He guided Abraham to the Promised Land.

My friend Dennis Coleman tells about a woman he knew through an Internet forum for Christians who had met a man through the Internet and after a long time wanted to meet him in person. Many of those on the forum told her this was a bad idea; there were no safeguards, nothing to protect her if this man was not what he seemed. Dennis, though, took a much more sensible approach, and asked the woman what God was telling her to do. After all, we are always completely safe when we do what God directs, even if it appears otherwise, and we are never completely safe when we step outside God's will even if He protects us anyway. There are many "rules" in life that are good and true and useful, that are not God's answer to every situation that falls under them, and one of them is certainly do not meet strangers in unfamiliar places without making some sort of arrangements for your safety. That may be an excellent rule, but it's rather clear that precious little of the evangelism reported in the New Testament would have occurred had Phillip, Peter, Paul, and so many others followed it. My friend rightly thought that if God was telling this woman to meet this man, she should meet him, and if God was telling her not to do so, she should not. What was God telling her to do?

She had not asked God. She told Dennis this. She was willing to try to get the opinions of people she knew only over the Internet, but she was not willing to ask God what she should do. She did not ask God, she said, because she was afraid He would tell her not to go, and she did not want Him to tell her that.

In terms of guidance, Dennis astutely observed that perhaps she already had her answer, because if she thought God was going to tell her not to meet this man it might be that He was already telling her that and she was trying to ignore it. At the same time, he also saw the more serious issue. You say that you believe in God. Presumably that means that you trust God, and believe that God loves you and has your best interests in view in all He does. Yet right here, where it matters, you do not trust that God will direct you in the best course. Surely if God is telling you that you should not meet this man, He has a good reason for doing it. It might not be that He is preventing you from becoming a statistic, but it certainly is not that He is trying to keep you from finding happiness in life. Do you believe that He cares for you? Do you believe that He has your best interests in view? Do you believe that He actually does know what is best? If you are afraid that He will tell you not to do what you want to do, or to do what you do not want to do, then you do not really believe one of those truths. He doesn't care about you; or even though He cares, He has too much to do to worry about what matters to you, or needs to use you as a pawn in His game plan; or even if He does have your best interests in view, He does not really know what is best for you, or is unable to bring it about.

We come by those doubts honestly. After all, we are humans, and the children of humans, and none of us have had perfect parents, perfect spouses, or perfect friends. We have all been in situations where someone we thought ought to care truly did not. We have had those who cared about us be too busy to help us, or too focused on their own problems or interests to be concerned for our needs or wishes. We have all had parents or friends or loved ones who stood in our way with the best of intentions, telling us that they were acting for our own good as they blocked our careers or our relationships or any of so many things. We have come to believe that no one really knows what is best for us better than we. No one has the same care for us as we do, no one is as attentive to our needs as we are, and no one can see what is best for us like we can. We do not trust anyone so much as we trust ourselves. It is not natural to trust someone else like that, at least, not where it matters.

Thus we always limit our trust. We trust our doctors as long as they are telling us what we want to believe, but as soon as we don't like what we hear we go looking for a second opinion. We trust that our parents care for us, but let them try to influence our love lives and they will almost invariably have the reverse effect of what they intend. We trust our teachers to be right about most of what they teach, but let them contradict what we thought we knew and we'll be demanding proof. Trust has its limits.

We also trust God, but our trust has its limits. If we think our happiness lies in one direction, and He says we should not go there, do we trust Him, or go with our own thoughts and feelings? If we have outlined our own career path to success, and He calls us elsewhere, do we trust Him, or stick to our plans? If we have found our perfect match and God says this is not the one for us, do we trust Him, or plan the wedding?

The very foundation of our salvation lies in these questions. If God says that He loves us and wants to accept us by His mercy and grace, not because we deserve it but because we know we do not, do we trust Him, or do we struggle to make something of ourselves so we can stand before Him and tell Him that we really are good people who deserve an eternal reward in His presence because of all the good things we have done? We are called to trust Him for this, to believe that He is embracing us as we are, loving the dirty little creatures He has made. To tell Him that we deserve any good from Him is to insult Him.

That salvation is only the beginning of our relationship with Him, but it reveals the essential quality of that relationship. We did not begin by the

Spirit so as to be perfected by the flesh.[42] God did not say that we should trust Him to save us but then that we should trust ourselves for everything else. There really *is* nothing else. It is all about our salvation. Our relationships, our careers, our lives are all entirely about whether we trust God. What we call salvation is only the starting point of salvation, the entrance into the relationship of trusting God that then characterizes the rest of our lives. Did you shake hands with God and say, "I'm pleased to meet You, now if You will excuse me I have to get back to running my life"? Or did you grasp His hand and say, "I am so glad You have come, here are the books, I look forward to seeing what You do to turn this life around and make it work"? Only the latter is really trusting God.

That trust then continues through our lives. "Do you trust me?" God asks, as our assets dwindle and we cannot find work. "Do you trust me?" He calls, as we find ourselves lost in an unfamiliar and dangerous area late at night. "Do you trust me?" He says, as our lives appear to be collapsing around us.

As we hesitantly answer, "Yes," He works the miracles. They are not always the miracles we expected or wanted, but they prove to us once again that He has everything in control, and He is working for our good.[43] The real miracle is not so much that we come through safely, that He may heal or restore, or that He provides for our needs. The real miracle is that we have found Him trustworthy, and so we trust Him more.

---

[42] Galatians 3:3
[43] Romans 8:28

I shared this story and these thoughts with a young woman who asked about worry. Her question at first was whether it was always a sin to worry, but as her thoughts unfolded the nature of her worry became clear. She was facing some potentially serious health problems, and thought she might die. For herself, that was not a problem; she was confident in her place in heaven with Christ. However, the elder of her two children was not yet in grade school, and she worried about what would become of them if they grew up without her.

I called her attention to Paul's thoughts in the first chapter of Philippians, where he suggests that it would be better for him if he were to die and be with the Lord, but that they apparently still needed him so he was going to have to stay here on earth for yet a while longer.[44] What was true for Paul and the Philippians was true for this woman and her children: as long as they needed her, she would be there for them. That did not mean that there was no chance that she would die, but rather that she could be confident that whether she lived or died, God was taking care of her little ones. If He needed her to be the instrument of that care, she would be there. If He took her out of their lives, she would know that He could see how to care for them better without her there. Statistically we know that children who lose a parent do not do as well in human terms as those who grow up in two-parent households; we, though, were not concerned with human terms so much as with God's work in the lives of those little ones, and He would guide their

---

[44] Philippians 1:21ff

lives through what they needed, watching over them and meeting their needs, whether their mother was with them or not. Ultimately, she had no need to worry, because the care of her children rested not with her but with God, Who would continue to care for them just as He was caring for her.[45]

All of this comes back to that mustard seed. Jesus said that if we had faith the size of a mustard seed, we could move mountains[46] and rip out trees[47] that were in our way. Yet what does it mean, to have faith as a grain of mustard? What is it about mustard seeds that matters in this context?

Jesus used that same image, the picture of the grain of mustard, in another parable.[48] He said that the Kingdom of Heaven was just like this mustard seed, and He explained this. The mustard seed, He said, is a tiny seed, the smallest seed known at that time. The mustard tree from which the seed comes is a great spreading tree, a place where flocks of birds will roost. Yet the tree comes from the seed. That tiny little grain, about the size of a crystal of sand or salt, contains within it the potential to grow, to become that huge tree.

---

[45] It may sound callous to suggest to the mother of young children that her children might not need her. I recognized this at the time, and made the point that I did not mean to be harsh. She understood, and saw from this that God's love was perhaps a bit bigger than she had realized, because she could trust Him to care for her children just as she trusted Him to care for her.
[46] Matthew 17:20
[47] Luke 17:6
[48] Matthew 13:31f, Luke 13:19

In the same way, that tiniest bit of faith that trusts God for the seemingly smallest things, that says, "All right, I'll follow you and see where You are leading me," as Abraham did when he left for the promised land, is the starting point. It is enough faith that God can take it and nurture it and cause it to grow into a great tree, faith enough that nature itself must give way for your faith. Trust God for the smallest thing that comes to you, and eventually you will know that He is completely and absolutely trustworthy, and you will trust Him for the greatest, the miraculous. Accept that He will do those little things He says He will do, and as He proves Himself there, you will find it easier to trust Him for bigger and greater things, as your faith grows from a speck to a tall sturdy pillar supporting a vast spreading canopy.

Thus it is as was said in the introduction, that God is reaching out, asking, "Do you trust me?" We take His hand with a tentative, "Yes", and learn trust from there.

Breaking the Law

Israel, pursuing a law of righteousness, did not arrive at that law. Why? Because they did not pursue it by faith, but as though it were by works.[49]

There is something very peculiar about the book of Genesis when we consider it within its context as the first of the five books of the Law of Moses. We call those the Pentateuch, the Five Books; the Jews call them Torah, Law. Collectively they give us what we think is the pattern for how to be pleasing to God. Since we call it "Law", we expect it to be filled with statutes, statements saying what must and must not be done. As a collection, it does not disappoint, as it contains much that fits this model. However, the first book, Genesis, does not seem like Law at all. It seems much more like the stories of men who trusted God. We might easily call it the first Book of Faith. Commandments are few and far between in its pages.

If we continue reading past Genesis into Exodus, we have to read fairly far before we come to anything resembling what we would call "law". We have the story of the birth of Moses, his flight from Egypt, his experience at the burning bush, his return with Aaron, his confrontations before Pharaoh, the plagues, the Passover, the Exodus itself, the crossing of the Red Sea, and then finally we reach the mountain and get our first commandments. For books that are supposed to be

---

[49] Romans 9:31f

about Law, they seem to spend a great deal of time talking about something entirely different.

Of course, we are so accustomed to thinking of this as The Law that we ignore this. We need to put it in perspective, perhaps, so we can see it. Imagine that you signed up for a five-day seminar about United States Federal Law, and the speaker spent the first day lecturing about the Pilgrims and Puritans and the colonists in Virginia and the settlement of New Amsterdam, and the various charters and founding of each of the thirteen colonies, and then the next morning began with a lesson about the American Revolutionary War. You would have to conclude one of two things. Either your teacher is completely incompetent and has no idea how to teach Federal Law, or somehow all of this history is essential to understanding the material to be covered over the next three and a half days.

It is the same problem we face with the Pentateuch. The first book and almost half of the second[50] do not contain rules or commandments, but are the stories of acts of faith, of men who believed what God said and acted accordingly. We must then decide whether Moses, and by inference God, really had no idea how to write law, or whether somehow all of this that comes at the beginning is essential to understanding the rest.

---

[50] The Ten Commandments are introduced as the first commandments in Exodus 20 of a 40-chapter book, although there are a few points raised before that.

46

Reflect on this for a moment. It appears that the first thirty percent of the instruction in Law is comprised of lessons about faith. Since we would all hesitate to say that God did not know what He was doing when He ordered these books, it seems that these stories about faith must be the starting point, the fundamental lessons on which any correct understanding of the Law itself must be built. In order to understand the Law, you must start, it would seem, by understanding faith.

We have already looked at some of the examples and lessons of faith that are contained in that material. We have seen that God was never pleased by manipulative obedience to rules, and was always pleased by those who simply trusted Him to accept them despite their flaws. Everything in those stories seems to be completely contrary to a view of obeying the rules to earn God's acceptance.

This really does make sense, even from a human perspective. Picture these two different sons for a moment. The first says, "Dad, I took out the trash, cleaned my room, washed the floor, and did everything you told me to do, and now as you promised you have to buy me that game I want, so let's go get it." The second says, "Dad, I'm really sorry that I can't seem to be the perfect son, and I know I didn't do everything you asked, but I really do love you, and I'm happy just to be your son, and hope you'll overlook my flaws." Which one gets the game? Do you really want a relationship with your son that is based on him doing what you want so that you will have to do what he wants, like some business contract? Would you not rather have a son who loves you, and is happy just to know that you love him, one who wishes he were more pleasing to you but can't do everything you expect? Sure, we would all like the perfect son who does everything we want *and* loves us expecting nothing from us, but as between the two, the son who does what we ask in order to get what he wants is not the loving son, and not the son we are likely to embrace warmly, to whom we would say, "I would love to buy you something you'll enjoy, so let's go look at games." When that other boy says, "You don't have to do that, Dad," we know that there is love there. We say, "I know, son, but I want to do it anyway."

That is the kind of children God wants, people who love Him and are happy just to know that He loves us. Those are the children on whom He wants to lavish His gifts—not the manipulative ones who expect to be compensated for each chore they complete.

This is what that first book and a half of the Law teaches us, that God wants faith, wants trust and love from people, and not some sort of contract in which He is paying for obedience with rewards. Abel, Noah, Abraham, Isaac, Jacob, Joseph, Moses, all of them teach the same lesson, that it is not keeping the rules that makes one right with God, but trusting and loving God.

So then, what's the point of the rest of the books? Obviously, the law contains many commandments, statutes, ordinances, whatever you would call them. If pleasing God is not about being obedient to the rules, what is the point of the rules? The stuff about faith might come first, but the stuff about rules seems to dominate the text. At some point it must be about rules, right? How do they fit?

Paul makes an astute observation about this in Romans. He says that the Israelites pursued a law of righteousness but did not obtain it *because they did not pursue it by faith, but as though it were by works.*[51] That should have clued us to the truth of the matter, but we didn't understand that, either, in the main. What did Paul mean about pursuing a law by faith and not by works? Isn't the keeping of a law essentially about works?

There is a very interesting point to notice about the Ten Commandments and the Law that follows from it, which most of us fail to notice because it comes from an earlier place and time. The text of Exodus 20 takes the form of what scholars of ancient types of literature[52] call a *suzerainty treaty.* To understand this, we have to understand something of the politics of the age.

In the ancient middle east, there were big kingdoms and little kingdoms, and they were always at war. The little kingdoms would fight each other, and then whoever won would demand tribute from the loser, until the loser decided to fight again and try to reverse the situation. We see this happening much in what we call the historic books, from Judges through Chronicles. However, the little kingdoms were all sandwiched between the big ones—Babylon, Assyria, Egypt. These bigger kingdoms didn't play the game the same way.

---

[51] Romans 9:32
[52] Usually called "form critics".

49

When they decided to conquer you, they were taking over, and if they won, you might just cease to exist. There was little hope of turning the tables in that situation, and little hope of winning.

The little kingdoms had a chance, though, because they were, after all, the buffer zones between the big ones. Thus if one big kingdom threatened to conquer you, you sent emissaries to another big kingdom in the opposite direction, in essence explaining that you were in danger of becoming subsumed by their rival, which would mean that the first empire would then be bigger, have more resources and more manpower, and would have moved its borders that much closer to the second. The second empire had a real interest in preventing that from happening, at least in ensuring that if this little country wasn't going to become its own province, it didn't become part of the opposing empire. Thus the empire to which you appealed would send out its armies, rattle some sabers, maybe fight a skirmish here or there, and the first empire, who really wasn't looking for a fight with one of the big guys, would back down and leave the little country alone for a while.

That's when the suzerainty treaty comes into existence. The suzerain is the king of the empire that just saved your neck. He, or usually his general, now enters your capital, welcomed as the deliverer he is. He unrolls his scroll, and makes his announcement. These are his terms.

The form of the treaty begins with a statement of all the wonderful things the suzerain has already done in delivering the small country

50

from its oppressor. This often goes on for pages, and is usually exaggerated. Eventually, though, it gets to the point. The point is, *because I have already done all these wonderful things for you, out of your gratitude you are going to do these things for me*. Thus asking one of the big countries to come protect you from another was something of a risk, because it wasn't until after you'd received the protection that you were told the price. However, at least you remained your own sovereign country.

With this in view, we can turn our attention to the giving of the Law. The first words are, "I am the Lord your God who brought you out of the land of Egypt, out of the house of slavery."[53] That's the entire first part of the treaty. That's all God says about His side of the deal—and yet for those who were there to hear those words first spoken, it was enough. They had lived through it, seen the plagues, crossed the parted sea, eaten the miraculous food, drunk from the rocks, and were now a free people sitting at the base of this mountain. We, and their descendants, could discover all the important details of that deliverance in the nineteen chapters of the book that preceded this. God did not have to brag about what He did, or exaggerate it. He said, "This is what I did for you."

The next words are, "You will have no other gods before me."[54] Those are the first words of the second part of the treaty. What, though, is that second part? That's the part where the treaty says,

---

[53] Exodus 20:2
[54] Exodus 20:3

because I have done these wonderful things for you, you, *because of your gratitude*, will do this for me. The entirety of the Law, all the commandments, were given as God's explanation of what Israel should do to express their gratitude for what He had already done.

That is why Paul can make the statement he made. The Law was never about what to do to earn God's favor; it was about what to do to show man's appreciation for God's favor already granted. The Jews thought that they could manipulate God, that by performing the sacrifices and keeping the festivals and obeying the various regulations they would force God to treat them favorably. Paul says that's all backwards. It is because God has already treated us favorably that we respond by doing all those things the law commends.

That is also why Paul tells us that God set the Law aside.[55] Things had gotten so confused and turned around that those who really wanted to come to God in faith thought it was hopeless, that they could only come to God by keeping the law perfectly. That which was supposed to bring life, by showing us how to celebrate God's love for us, became a source of death, by burdening us with impossible requirements.[56] It had to be removed, so we could learn to celebrate the love of God. We might have done that by keeping the Law. David understood that; that's why the Psalms speak of loving God's law,[57] and David danced before the

---

[55] Romans 3:21
[56] Romans 7:10
[57] Psalm 119:97, 113, 163, 165

Lord.[58] Yet by the time Saul of Tarsus saw Steven stoned, the Pharisees had become so locked into the idea that Law was what you did to make God accept you that the Christian message of God accepting sinners was regarded blasphemy. The entire purpose of the law as a means for Israel to express their gratitude to the God who had delivered them and made them His people was in danger of being lost.

God's solution to the problem was to reach out and save the gentiles, people who were not party to that treaty and so had no obligation to keep that law, and to announce that He was accepting them in love and making no demands on them. Let the gentiles express their gratitude however they thought best. The law would not matter to them. It didn't work for Israel, so it would not be applied to the gentiles.

And so it was faith that saved the gentiles, just as it was faith that saved Israel, that willingness to trust God, followed by the joyous expression of gratitude to the One Who worked the miracles that delivered us.

---

[58] II Samuel 6:14ff

Faith of the Lawgiver

Moses was faithful as a servant....[59]

    The eleventh chapter of Hebrews provides a list of people who are examples of faith. We have looked at several of these; most of them are mentioned briefly, leaving the reader to learn about their faith. It is not surprising that the one most discussed there is Abraham,[60] the father of the faithful, the head of the household of God on earth. What perhaps might be surprising, though, is that the person who ranks second in the amount said about him there, and indeed the only other person to receive more than passing notice, is Moses,[61] the lawgiver.

    This in itself should catch our attention. If the Law is about salvation by works, how can the one who delivered the Law to God's people have been an example of faith? Should he not have been an example of works righteousness?

    That immediately runs us into trouble. As a young man, Moses fled from Egypt because he was wanted for murder,[62] and the account suggests that the charges may have been valid. We might claim that his act was justified under a defense of third persons notion, if we assert that the Egyptian he killed was beating the Israelite he saved severely enough that death was likely, but we don't have

---

[59] Hebrews 3:5
[60] Hebrews 11:8-12, 17-19
[61] Hebrews 11:23-29
[62] Exodus 2:12, 15

proof of that. Having fled, he married the daughter of a man who was not circumcised,[63] not one of God's people. We are told that the man was a Midianite priest,[64] which makes him a descendant of Abraham by his later wife Keturah,[65] and likely a worshipper of God,[66] but not one of the nation of Israel. We also know that Moses did not circumcise his two sons when they were infants; his wife had to do it to save his life later when God was angry with him about that.[67] Moses was not the paragon of legal virtue and example of righteous living one expects from the one saved by his own works. Certainly there are worse people in the world, and certainly God forgave his sins, but that he needed forgiveness at all seems to disqualify him from the role.

We have already seen that the Law was given not as a means to acceptance by God but as a means of expressing the joy of that acceptance. Moses writes and says many things in the Law which might cause us to believe that he understood this as being about works righteousness, and the Pharisees of Jesus' day certainly thought that was the intent. Can we know that Moses understood this to be an expression of faith rather than a means to God's acceptance?

---

[63] Exodus 2:21

[64] Exodus 2:16

[65] Genesis 25:1ff

[66] This is on the assumption that Abraham taught his younger children about God, and this knowledge was passed through the generations. This does not mean that the Midianite people were also faithful to God, but that at least some of them knew of Him.

[67] Exodus 4:24ff

If Moses himself came to God on the basis of trust, then it must be that trust in God was the path to righteousness of the Lawgiver, and also in the Law.

The author of Hebrews begins with the faith of Moses' parents.[68] There is much that can be learned from this, as they struggled to find a way to obey Pharaoh's command that Israelite boy babies should be thrown into the Nile river, while at the same time honoring God by not killing a baby. Their solution is ingenious.[69] They kept the boy hidden for three months, fed and warm and growing to a point where he stood a chance of surviving alone for at least a day, then put him in the river, but with two precautions. First, he was placed in a basket which would keep him afloat and dry, as long as it remained upright. Second, he was put in the shallows among the reeds, so that the current could not carry him into the deeper parts of the river. All they could do after that is trust God to care for their son, but God honored that faith and saved the boy. In the end, Moses' mother was paid to care for the boy she had refused to kill, and by the people who had ordered her to kill him.

It is the next point that the author of Hebrews mentions that shows us the faith of Moses. He sided with the Israelite slaves against their Egyptian masters.[70] He could easily have accepted his comfortable place as son of Pharaoh's daughter,

---

[68] Hebrews 11:23
[69] The details are in Exodus 2:2ff
[70] Hebrews 11:24ff

in essence the grandchild of one Pharaoh and the nephew of the next. His parents, whose faith had saved him as an infant, had apparently impressed something of that faith on him in the short time they had to raise him. He believed it was better to be counted with the people of God in their slavery than to be a member of one of the most powerful royal families in the world at that time. He made that choice.

That choice cost. He lost his position in the Egyptian court, but was not immediately recognized as a leader in Israel. This led to a period of doubt, ultimately to a moment when God's audible voice coming from the fire in the bush that was not burning[71] was not enough to persuade him. He raised his doubts, and discovered that God had answers to all his questions. He raised his inadequacies, and God gave him someone to work with him, someone who had the gifts Moses lacked. He raised his fears, and God gave him the tools to do the job, miracles which Moses could perform at will.

It took much to convince Moses that God was going to use him to deliver Israel from Egypt. Once he was convinced, however, there was no stopping him. He trusted God to work a string of miracles,[72] challenging the Egyptian authorities, customs, and religions, and demanding that God's people be set free.

---

[71] Exodus 3:2
[72] Exodus 5:1ff. The specific details of how the plagues related to the power of the Egyptian gods is beyond the scope of this book.

The author of Hebrews skips all of this. He jumps from the decision Moses made to be numbered among God's people to the moment of the Passover.[73] In doing so, he brings out the significance of this one event. It was here that all of Israel was saved by their faith. Moses had faith, and that faith brought death to the enemies of God's people. However, it was the faith in each Israelite household that saved them from that same destruction.

At Passover, Moses announced that the destroyer was coming, who would kill the firstborn males of all the Egyptians.[74] This was the most powerful miracle he had worked, and it boggles the mind to attempt to understand it. Modern scientists attempt to explain the plagues, and some very credible efforts have connected each to the next in a natural chain of events. However, no natural disaster, no disease, no parasite could do what Moses said God was about to do. Death would come to many, not randomly, but specifically. Only males would die; no one lost a daughter or a mother or a sister to this. Only first born males would die; no second sons lost their lives. Yet it was not limited by age, as whether the boy was two months or twenty years old he died if he was the firstborn male. It was not limited to humans, either, as scripture tells us that the firstborn of all the livestock also died.[75]

---

[73] Hebrews 11:28
[74] Exodus 11:4ff
[75] Exodus 12:29

Consider Moses' faith here. He dared to announce this would happen, an event we still cannot explain beyond saying God did it. He said it was going to happen, because God told him it was going to happen. He then said that there was a way to save your own child, because God told him that the firstborn sons of the Israelites would be saved if they did as instructed.[76]

Now consider the faith of the Israelites. They had to believe, first, that God was going to kill all the firstborn males, and only the firstborn males, in the entire land of Egypt. This incredible and inexplicable miracle was going to happen. If you did not believe it was going to happen, there would be absolutely no reason to go through all that trouble to prevent it. A lamb is a valuable animal. The work of slaughtering it is messy, and doing it at the door of the home means there is going to be a lot of cleanup to do the next day. There are many reasons why this entire ritual of protection is a bad idea, and the only reason to do it is that you believe you need protection from this destroyer Moses says God says is about to sweep through the land killing all the firstborn males.

More than that, though, each Israelite family had to slaughter its own lamb, place the blood on its own doors, stay inside its own home. In essence, every Israelite family was trusting God to perform a miracle for them. It was not because Moses prayed that the destroyer passed over my house, but because I made the sacrifice, I kept my family indoors that night, I served the meal and placed the

---

[76] Exodus 12:13

blood on the lintel and doorposts and in the basin. I performed that miracle, the miracle that saved my son. Moses had the faith to tell me that this would work, but it was my faith, my trust that if God told Moses this would protect my son, I needed to do this.

Moses gave faith to the entire nation of Israel. Not one Israelite boy died that night, because every Israelite family believed that God was going to send the destroyer, and that by following God's instructions they would be protected from it.

Thus at that moment Israel was saved by faith. That is, because they trusted what God had told them through Moses, they lived.

The author of Hebrews is not finished telling us about the faith of Moses, though. Passover may have been the greatest and most important miracle Moses would perform, but shortly after that he would be called upon to trust God for a much more impressive miracle. Israel was to cross the Red Sea on dry ground.[77] A generation later, when Joshua led the nation against Jericho, it was this miracle that had reached the ears of the people of the land, and for this reason fear gripped their enemies.[78]

Israel was following God's manifestation in a pillar of fire.[79] The Egyptian army decided to give

---

[77] Hebrews 11:29
[78] Joshua 2:9ff
[79] Exodus 13:21

chase.[80] Suddenly the fleeing people came face to face with an unanticipated obstacle. God had led them to the shore of a vast sea. Panic ensued, and they blamed Moses.

Moses' response at this moment is remarkable. He tells them, "Stand by and see the salvation of the Lord," and "the Egyptians you see today you will never see again forever."[81] He had no idea what was going to happen, but he knew that God was going to deliver them. He trusted that God would do it.

Meanwhile, he was already praying for an answer. We know that he was already praying for an answer, because God asks him why he is asking.[82] Moses wanted God to tell him what to do, but God thought the answer was obvious. Remember, Israel has been following this column of smoke and fire by which God was leading them. It had brought them to the edge of the water. That is where their path led, and they should be following it.

The sea was in their *path* at this point, but it was not in their *way*. God knew it was there, and God knew that it was not going to be an obstacle for them. He was already directing them toward the edge of the water, and His answer to Moses amounts to asking why they have stopped following. It's a bit like Peter Pan flying out the window, then asking Wendy why she's not

---

[80] Exodus 14:5ff
[81] Exodus 14:13
[82] Exodus 14:15

following him. In this case, though, God knows that the water is not going to prevent them from crossing.

At this moment, Israel sees death coming from behind and death standing in front of them, and they do not know what to do. Yet they trusted God when He reassured them that they were to walk into the sea. What they thought was the obstacle that would kill them proved instead to be the tool of their deliverance from the real danger, as they crossed that sea. The water was to their left and their right as they crossed,[83] but then the Egyptians were buried in it,[84] never to be seen alive again, as Moses had promised.

God expected Israel to trust Him for this, and once He reassured them, they did. God's first instruction to Moses was not how to move the obstacle out of the way, but to tell the people to keep walking toward it. It was only after the people were told to keep moving that God told Moses to stretch his staff over the water and part it.[85] Israel had to trust that God was going to bring them across that sea before He told anyone how He was going to do it.

Thus again Israel was saved by faith, by trusting God that the path He had chosen would be safe, and that the obstacles that looked fatal would be moved. This miracle is celebrated centuries later

---

[83] Exodus 14:22, 29
[84] Exodus 14:28
[85] Exodus 14:15f

in the Psalms.[86] It was remembered with joy. Again it was faith that saved Moses and all of Israel.

Thus when we come at last to the giving of the Law, we see the form of the suzerainty treaty. We see God, with a very few words, saying, *This is the wonderful thing I did for you. You trusted me to deliver you, and I did. Now this is what you are going to do for me, out of your gratitude for that deliverance.*

Christians have a great deal of difficulty understanding how the Law relates to the Christian life. On the one hand, it appears from passages in Galatians[87] and Romans[88] and elsewhere that Christians have absolutely no obligation to keep the Law of Moses at all. On the other hand, it is equally clear that we are expected to live decent moral lives, and that the Old Testament, the only Bible the New Testament church had, is our Bible. How is this reconciled?

God expected Israel to express its gratitude to Him for saving them from Egypt and making them His people and blessing them, by keeping the Law He had given them. It is easy to see how in subsequent generations this was forgotten. Time and time again the Law was abandoned by a people who simply were not terribly grateful for what God had done for their ancestors. Sometimes they returned to Him for forgiveness, and at those times they expressed their gratitude by keeping the Law.

---

[86] Psalm 66, 74, 78, 106, 114, 136
[87] see the author's book *About the Fruit*
[88] see the author's book *What Does God Expect?*

However, a separate idea emerged, one which saw the Law not as an expression of gratitude but as a list of requirements, a way to be accepted by God instead of a way to express the joy of having been accepted. By the time Jesus came, this view was the majority position. Most people believed that to be pleasing to God you had to keep the requirements of the Law. The few, the Pharisees, then believed that they were doing so. The many, the commoners, believed that God did not care for them because they did not measure up to the standard He imposed.

Part of the message of the gospel is this: forget about trying to keep the Law as a way of winning God's favor. That was never its purpose, and to use it that way is to misuse it and miss the point. This has become so confused, let's forget about the Law altogether and get back to doing what it was the Law was supposed to enable: showing our gratitude to God by acting like His chosen and redeemed people.

That was all the Law was ever intended to do, to give Israel a picture of how a grateful chosen and redeemed people living in their time and place ought to act. What does it mean for us? It means that as God's chosen and redeemed people, we are invited to show our gratitude to Him by acting like His children, the chosen and redeemed of the Lord. The Law is a picture of some of what that might mean, but the starting point for the Law is not a set of rules for how to act but a picture of faith, of trust in the God who loves us as we are and asks only that we love Him in return, and act like we love and trust Him.

That was what the Lawgiver knew. That was why He gave the Law. Even the Law was always about faith.

What About Doubt?

I do believe; help my unbelief.[89]

We have already noted that the Old Testament is filled with those who by trusting God received their deliverance. Abel, Noah, Abraham, and Moses all point to faith as the way of salvation in their time, just as it is in ours. Yet few believers never doubt. Trust is a demanding capacity. Some will not ride the more thrilling amusement park rides, not because these are not fun, nor because they believe them dangerous, but simply because they do not have enough trust to overcome their doubts. If that perfect trust were required perfectly, none of us would be numbered among the elect.

Yet even among the great examples of faith there were those with doubts. We have seen how God built Abraham's faith a bit at a time, but with Moses it was different. We saw that when God told Moses it was time to do what Moses had already failed to do years before, Moses argued. He doubted that God could use him for the task for which God had made, prepared, and called him. It took some convincing.

The catalogue of the faithful in Hebrews 11 contains others who are prominent in their doubts; from their stories we can learn much about faith.

Gideon[90] is an excellent example of someone who doubted. His story opens with this

---

[89] Mark 9:24

paragon of trust in God threshing grain in a wine vat.[91] This is actually a very funny image that we miss because we have lost that primitive agricultural context. When wheat is harvested, the grains themselves are wrapped in light paper-like shells called chaff, a bit like the inner cover on peanuts. These are easily removed by hand, but that doing each one individually would take a very long time. Thus the easy way to do it without modern machinery is to climb to the top of a hill where there is a stiff breeze, and rub handfuls of grain between your palms. The heavy grain falls into a pan on the ground while the breeze blows away the chaff.

Of course, there is very little breeze in a wine vat, and what little there is tends to travel in circles, trapped by the rounded walls. Gideon must be sitting there blowing on the falling grain to carry away the chaff. He is afraid that the Midianites will see him working if he does it the easy way, and they will come take his grain from him. The man at this point is an example of caution and wariness.

This is the man to whom the angel appears. This is the man the angel hails as a "valiant warrior".[92]

Given this image, it is no wonder that Gideon asked the angel if he hadn't gotten the wrong address. Gideon perceived himself as an unimportant younger son in an unimportant family

---

[90] Hebrews 11:32
[91] Judges 6:11
[92] Judges 6:12

in an unimportant tribe.[93] Yet God was willing to take the time to persuade and encourage the faith he had, and when Gideon asked how it could be that God truly favored them when God had not sent miraculous deliverance from the Midianites, the angel said, You, Gideon, are the miracle. God has sent you.[94]

Where is Gideon's faith here? He has that tiny seed of faith. He already believes that God is able to deliver Israel; he only questions why God has not chosen to do so.[95] He believes that God can work this deliverance, but doubts that God might actually be choosing him through whom to do it.[96] Once God confirms all this to him by a minor miracle, he proceeds to do what God has instructed.

However, he is not finished doubting. He tears down his father's pagan altar[97] and sees what might to him have been the greater miracle of his father coming to his defense.[98] He raises an army and prepares to attack the enemy. Then he doubts again. He does not doubt whether God can do this; he doubts whether he got the message right. He says to God, "If you are going to do what you said you were going to do," and asks God to confirm the message. He puts out his fleece.[99]

---

[93] Judges 6:15
[94] Judges 6:14
[95] Judges 6:13
[96] Judges 6:17
[97] Judges 6:25ff
[98] Judges 6:31
[99] Judges 6:36ff

69

Many Christians point, directly or indirectly, to this act of Gideon. We call it *fleecing*, and connect it to any prayer that asks God to confirm His direction through a tangible sign. It can be a useful practice. However, it is driven by doubt, not faith. It is a way of questioning whether God meant what He said.

God respects Gideon's doubts, and confirms His instructions by the double sign of the fleece—first dew on the wool but not the floor, then dew on the floor but not the wool. Gideon is persuaded, and prepares to fight.

However, Gideon's doubt has cost something. He knew that God had called him to defeat Midian, but he wanted that last bit of reassurance to bolster his confidence before he led his thirty-two thousand soldiers into war.[100] God gave him that reassurance, clearly and powerfully, and he is now ready. However, it is at this point that God demands more of His chosen servant. You did not trust Me, Gideon, but now you do. You have thirty-two thousand men, but you wanted me to assure you that I was with you. Now that you believe that, you do not need so many men. Then, in two sweeping steps, God reduces that army from five digits to three, leaving His chosen general a mere three hundred men with whom to assault the vast Midianite forces.

God will give you the reassurance you need. He will build that faith, taking you from uncertainty to confidence. However, when God gives you more

---

[100] Judges 7:3

70

reason to trust Him, He will in turn expect you to trust Him more. God does not waste his assurances on people who do not need them. He gives confidence to those who will face obstacles, and greater confidence to those for whom the obstacles will be greater. The odds were against Gideon from the start, as he was facing at least one hundred thirty-five thousand trained soldiers with a hastily scrounged militia about one quarter of that, but with the assurance that God was going to win this he no longer cared about the odds. Once he no longer cared about the odds, they skyrocketed. God raised Gideon's faith from that place where he was uncertain about four against one to the place where he believed that the fact God said He was going to win this was enough, and then said if that were true, five hundred to one is just as certain as four to one.

Gideon said yes. Gideon recognized that the time for doubt was over, and that if he could trust God to defeat Midian, the numbers on his side did not matter.

He was not quite finished doubting, though. We know this because God recognized it. When the time came for Gideon to attack, God gave him one last shot of confidence. If you have any doubt, God said, do this now.[101] Gideon did it. He certainly would not have gone to the enemy camp had he not trusted that God would protect him; however, he would not have gone there to have his doubts resolved if he had had no more doubts.

---

[101] Judges 7:10

God then encouraged Gideon through a dream.[102] This dream was not his dream, nor was it the dream of one of his friends or family members, nor one of his commanders, nor a prophet of Israel. It was, rather, the dream of a Midianite soldier which Gideon overheard being recounted to another Midianite soldier, and their explanation of it, that God had given victory over them, the Midianites, to Gideon and his army. Gideon's last doubts are resolved.

God recognizes that we doubt. He responds to our doubts with such assurances as will build our faith. Having done this, though, he then expects us to act on that faith. If God wants you to trust Him for *this*, whatever *this* is, and you ask Him to prove Himself, He will do so; He will then expect you to trust Him for *this*, and *that*, and maybe *the other thing*. The more He does to resolve your doubts and build your faith, the more He expects you to trust Him.

Doubt then becomes the step toward trust. If we are willing to ask God to prove Himself in our doubts, we find that He brings us to the place where we can trust Him yet more.

---

[102] Judges 7:13ff

Works of Faith

Faith without works is dead.[103]

To this point all we have said about faith is that it is our capacity to trust God. Our salvation lies in our ability to trust Him to save us. Nothing we can do will add to or detract from this.

Yet it seems that the Bible still expects us to do something. How do we know what we should do? Also, if we are saved without reference to what we do, why should we bother to do anything at all?

In I Corinthians 10, Paul points to Israel as an example to avoid. He first observes that they were God's people in much the same way as we, having been through something like water baptism, something like Holy Spirit baptism, and then having partaken of holy food and holy drink. They had been saved, saved from Egypt. Yet they never entered the promised land, but instead died in the desert. We need to avoid what happened to them, he says, by committing ourselves to live lives devoted to God.

Most Christians reading this passage think that it means you can lose your salvation, just as those Israelites lost their salvation; but no one in Israel lost his salvation—they were saved from Egypt, and they never returned to Egypt. What did they lose? They lost the promised land—not their salvation, but the good which God had for them. So

---

[103] James 2:26

for us, isn't that heaven? No, it is not. We have already been given the adoption as sons and the pledge of our redemption, and we are going to heaven; but the Christian life is about living, about what we have now. Paul is not afraid that we whom God has saved will be eternally lost; we are already eternally saved. He is afraid that we will miss all the good which God has for us here and now, the abundant life of which Jesus spoke. Further, it isn't a matter of how do we get that, but rather a matter of how do we miss it, and the answer is we miss it by not pursuing that trust relationship with God.

This means that we find the wonderful life God has promised by trusting Him. Further, all of those examples we have examined from the Old Testament tell us how to trust Him, how to live Christian lives. We can think back through the book to this point, and find in each chapter clues to how we express our love for and trust in God.

We look back to the definition of faith, the assurance of things hoped for, the conviction of things not seen, and realize that we trust God by believing what He tells us about the world, and believing that if he says the world is a particular way, and that certain things are good for us and others bad, that He is right. We realize that by doing the things God says are good, we will have better lives, and by doing the things God says are wrong, we will bring suffering on ourselves and others. It is not that God is a killjoy trying to keep us from enjoying life; it's that God knows what choices lead to the more joyful and more pleasurable life, and by following His advice we will find that better life.

We see that we should not be like Adam, who was afraid of God. There is a fear of the Lord, an awe and reverence and astonishment at His greatness; Adam's fear, though, was a lack of trust, a belief that God was going to hurt him. God is not going to hurt us, and we need to understand that. Within that understanding we again discover that the things God asks of us are always for our good.

We discover with Abel that God can be trusted, that we can approach Him because He loves us, and accepts us despite our sinfulness and despite our sins. We are His children, and even when we have done wrong He still embraces us and tries to help us learn to do right. We do not manipulate God by what we do, but come to Him as we are.

We learn so much from Abraham. Abraham teaches us that wherever God sends us is a good place, and we should follow His leading. He tells us that we can trust God's promises, and rely on them, and that nothing God asks us to do will ever prevent God from fulfilling His promises to us. We learn that God does not ask more of us than that for which we are prepared, but He builds our faith as we trust Him.

We learn from Enoch that what matters is the pursuit of a close relationship with God, and that God welcomes that relationship, and even desires it. From Noah, we see that God will tell us what we need to do so that we will be prepared for what is to come.

Then as we read the Law we begin to see how we can express our love and trust by living good lives, lives framed on a moral understanding of how to show our love for others and so through that for God. We learn that doing good is not a way to earn God's favor but rather a way to show our love and faith. We see in the life of Moses the lawgiver how faith is expressed in trusting God, but also in doing as God tells us. We learn from Moses' parents about doing the right thing and being rewarded for it. We learn about making difficult choices that cost us position and wealth and favor, in order to be what God made us to be. We learn that when we do as God asks, He works miracles.

We learn from Gideon that we can trust God against incredible odds.

Again and again the heroes of the Old Testament show us that what God directs will bring us to the best life we can have. It might not always be the life we would have chosen; sometimes that life is not possible, and sometimes that life would not have been what we expected. We see that God was molding them, using them, blessing them, and in all ways bringing them to Himself.

Martin Luther once wrote, "Good works do not make a good person, but a good person does good works."[104] God has called us and made us

---

[104] Martin Luther, *A Treatise on Christian Liberty*, in <u>Three Treatises</u> (Philadelphia: Muhlenberg Press, 1943) 271, cited in *Scripture as the Real Presence of Christ*, speech by The Rev. Prof. Karl P. Donfried, Th.D., at the 2007 ELCA convention.

good people, and more than good people, His own children. We respond by acting like His children, members of His family, and showing the world how very much God's family cares for everyone, as our Father cares for them.

That is what we do. It is our response from the trust we have in God.

The Bigger Picture

...the Lamb slain before the foundation of the world.[105]

To this point all we have been talking about is trusting God, seeing how the saints of old did it and what it means to us. Perhaps, though, it's worth asking why we're trusting God, and what really is happening here.

For many Christians, the "big picture" which explains all of life goes something like this. God wanted company, so he created man to live in harmony with Him forever. Man, though, derailed this plan, eating the fruit of the tree of the knowledge of good and evil and so destroying his fellowship with God. God then had to initiate Plan B, the backup plan. He had to send Jesus to die to get man out of this mess man had created for himself, so that He could put everything back the way it was intended originally.

The problems with this explanation of the world are serious. I once received a letter from an atheist who used this view as proof that God did not exist. After all, either God could not foresee Adam's fall or He could not prevent it, and either way that meant God was impotent, and not God at all.

Besides, there are no good "Plan B's"; if they were good, they'd be Plan A. God does not

---

[105] Revelation 13:8

have backup plans, because God does not need backup plans. Everything is unfolding exactly as He foresaw, and all that happens is according to plan.

Fundamentally, you see, the notion of God sending Jesus to correct our unexpected mistake is flawed, and not at all what the Bible teaches. Jesus, we are told, was "the lamb slain *before the foundation of the world.*"[106] That is, before Adam fell, even before Adam had been created, even before there was light, already the price of our redemption had been paid through the crucifixion and resurrection which would appear in time yet thousands of years from that moment. This was not God's "plan B".

That, though, means that all of this actually is God's "fault", as it were. He could have prevented it—all the suffering, all the pain, all the death, all the tears; the famines and the earthquakes and the floods and the storms; the starving children and the dying elderly; the cruelty, the war, the bitterness. God could have avoided all this. He certainly could have seen that we were going to sin and suffer, and prevented it all. He did not need to create us; He did not need to create anything. Presumably, too, He could have found a way to create creatures who would not fall. He chose to do this, to make us, knowing that we were going to go through all of these terrible pains. He did this to us. It really is all His fault.

Why, then, did He do it?

---

[106] *ibid*

Somewhere before all time and space, in some sense we cannot understand outside all time and space, God existed. He existed in that state we call Trinity, three persons unified in one, in some way that we cannot completely understand or describe; but there was love within that union. God saw that it was good for there to be persons who shared love, and He wanted there to be more persons sharing more love. He wanted something we would call children, but children who knew Him and loved Him genuinely.

We know that He created the angels; we cannot say with certainty when He created them relative to when He created us, nor even whether that question makes sense. In the angels He had devoted servants—but even with the limited freedom He gave them, He did not get children, beings like Himself. He certainly knew that He was not going to get children that way. Perhaps He wanted devoted servants as well; perhaps they were made as a necessary step toward making us. Angels did not truly understand love.

Thus He created us, knowing that we would fall, and that because we fell we would suffer. That suffering is an essential part of the process. It is why we can learn love, and the angels cannot. We can take risks, trusting each other and being hurt for it, and learning to trust again. We can make sacrifices, giving up something we desire or accepting something we would avoid, for the sake of someone else. We can love, precisely because it costs something to do so. If it cost us nothing, we could not learn love.

Nor could we learn trust. If no one and nothing ever failed us, trust would not be an issue. It would be there, as simple as that. It is because of risk that trust has meaning; it is because of pain that risk has meaning.

God created Adam knowing that Adam would bring death into the world, along with all the pain and suffering which we experience, because it was the only way God could produce sons and daughters for Himself—beings who loved and trusted, because they understood that love and trust meant opening yourself to risk and pain. All of this suffering, all of this evil, has a purpose: it forms us into loving trusting children of God.

Then into this world God came, and showed us how to serve, how to sacrifice, how to suffer and even die for the sake of others. He showed us what love means. He always loved us, and He was always willing to suffer for us; but to suffer for us, He had to become like us, live in our world of pain, and take that pain upon Himself. He did more than that, but He did not do less than that.

Eventually the risk, the pain, the suffering, the evil will all be gone. We will live in a world in which there is only good. Yet we will have learned to love, to put the needs of others before our own, to serve and sacrifice and care about others. We will have grown beyond selfishness, but not beyond self awareness. God will have His children, beings who like Him love each other.

We live in the midst of the pain, and it is difficult for us to have a proper perspective on our own condition. God saw the end from the beginning. He knows, He knew, all that would happen if He spoke those first words, if He brought the universe into existence and placed man upon the earth. He counted the cost; He measured the suffering. He also sees the outcome, what we shall be. We have His assurance that the finished product is worth the cost, that the pain and effort that goes into making us His children is a price worth paying by us, by Him, by the universe, to have millions of children made in His image, sharing love with Him and with each other, for the eternity to come.

We trust that He is right. That is our faith.

About The Author

"M.J." has served as a Chaplain for over two decades, has two degrees in Biblical studies and a doctorate in law, and is the author of several books on theology, gaming, and time travel theory. He lives in southern New Jersey, "a stone's throw from the Delaware Bay if you're Sandy Koufax", with his wife Janet and periodic extended visits from his five sons, a couple daughters-in-law, and grandchildren. He can be found on Facebook and other social media platforms and through MJYoung.net, the Christian Gamers Guild, and Patreon.

More To Explore

Other books by Mark Joseph Young:

- **Why I Believe**
  A profoundly comprehensive yet highly accessible apologetics tour-de-force by one of today's greatest Christian authors.

- **The Essential Guide To Time Travel**
  M.J. takes on Hollywood's favorite science fiction tales with his characteristic logic.

More Dimensionfold Authors:

- **Individuality and Primal Unity**
  This three-volume set by Rev. Jim Willis explores the role of ego in spirituality, through the lenses of Snow White, Robin Hood, and Merlin

- **Authority And Kingdoms**
  A short principles-based ebook commentary on Matthew chapter 8 by Ken Goudsward

- **Magic In The Bible**
  Ken Goudsward explores the idea of ancient magic by looking at the ministries of Daniel, Joseph, Moses, and Jesus

Find all these and more at Dimensionfold.com

Reviews Needed

Many readers do not realize how important book reviews are in this fast-paced electronic marketplace.

By leaving a review, you can provide your honest opinion, help other potential readers find this book, and help the author maintain their online presence.

Please search Amazon and review this book today!

www.ingramcontent.com/pod-product-compliance
Lightning Source LLC
Chambersburg PA
CBHW051007140626
46546CB00016B/1285